Taiga Experiments

12 Science Experiments in One Hour or Less

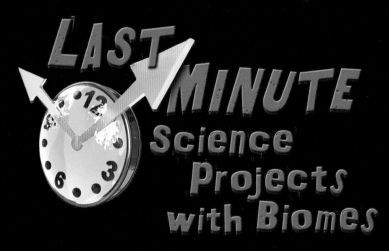

LAST MINUTE Science Projects with Biomes

ROBERT GARDNER

ILLUSTRATED BY TOM LABAFF

Enslow Publishers, Inc.
40 Industrial Road
Box 398
Berkeley Heights, NJ 07922
USA

http://www.enslow.com

Library of Congress Cataloging-in-Publication Data:
    Gardner, Robert, 1929–
    Taiga experiments : 12 science experiments in one hour or less / Robert Gardner.
        pages cm. — (Last minute science projects with biomes)
    Summary: "A variety of science projects related to the taiga biome that can be done in under an hour, plus a
        few that take longer for interested students"—Provided by publisher.
    Includes bibliographical references and index.
    ISBN 978-0-7660-5932-0
    1. Taigas—Experiments—Juvenile literature. 2. Biotic communities—Experiments—Juvenile literature. I.
        Title.
    QK938.T34G37 2015
    577.3'7—dc23
                                                2013010383

Future editions:
Paperback ISBN: 978-0-7660-5933-7
EPUB ISBN: 978-0-7660-5934-4
Single-User PDF ISBN: 978-0-7660-5935-1
Multi-User PDF ISBN: 978-0-7660-5936-8

Printed in the United States of America

052014 Lake Book Manufacturing, Inc., Melrose Park, IL

10 9 8 7 6 5 4 3 2 1

To Our Readers: We have done our best to make sure all Internet Addresses in this book were active and appropriate when we went to press. However, the author and the publisher have no control over and assume no liability for the material available on those Internet sites or on other Web sites they may link to. Any comments or suggestions can be sent by e-mail to comments@enslow.com or to the address on the back cover.

♻ Enslow Publishers, Inc., is committed to printing our books on recycled paper. The paper in every book contains 10% to 30% post-consumer waste (PCW). The cover board on the outside of each book contains 100% PCW. Our goal is to do our part to help young people and the environment too!

Illustration Credits: Tom LaBaff (www.tomlabaff.com)

Photo Credits: © 1999 Artville, LLC, p. 13; Courtesy of Environment Canada, p. 21; Robert Gardner, p. 25; © Thinkstock: Frank Hildebrand/iStock, p. 7; Oleg Rubik/iStock, p. 43; Purestock, p. 16; © Robert Blanchard/iStock, p. 44; TT/iStock, p. 5; Shutterstock.com: BMJ, p. 8; Dr. Morley Read, p. 45.

Cover Photos: Shutterstock.com: ©LehaKoK(dog track on snow); ©ILYA AKINSHIN(snowballs); ©Kichigin(snowflakes); ©Perutskyi Petro(pine tree); ©Tania Thomson(owl); ©Onur YILDIRIM(clock with yellow arrows); ©Thinkstock: Purestock(hare); Gert Very, Istock(woman)

Contents

🏅 Indicates an experiment that features an idea for a science fair or project

Are You Running Late?

If you have a science project that is due soon, maybe tomorrow, this book will help you. It has experiments about taiga (northern forest) biomes. Many of the experiments can be done in less than one hour. An estimate of the time needed is given for each experiment. Perhaps you have plenty of time to prepare for your next science project or fair. You can still use and enjoy this book.

Many experiments are followed by a "Keep Exploring" section. There you will find more ideas for science projects. The details are left to you, the young scientist. You can design and carry out your own experiments, **under adult supervision,** when you have more time.

For some experiments, you may need a partner to help you. Work with someone who likes to do experiments as much as you do. Then you will both enjoy what you are doing. **In this book, if any safety issues or danger is involved in doing an experiment, you will be warned. In some cases you will be asked to work with an adult. Please do so.** Don't take any chances that could lead to an injury.

Taiga Biomes

A biome is a region of Earth that has a particular climate. The plants and animals that live in a biome are quite similar all around the world. This book is about taiga biomes, also called boreal forests or northern coniferous forests. But there are other biomes. Earth's land biomes also include deserts, tundra, grasslands, rain forests, and temperate forests.

Taiga biomes extend around the Northern Hemisphere. They are found between tundra to the north and grasslands or temperate forests to the south. In general, they lie between 45 and 65 degrees north latitude. (A look at a world map or globe will reveal why there are no taiga biomes in the Southern Hemisphere.)

Taiga biomes receive between 12 and 33 inches of precipitation a year. That is approximately the same amount as grassland biomes. However, they

The taiga is also called a northern coniferous forest.

are wetter and colder than grasslands. Winter temperatures range between −45° and −1°C (−49° to 30°F). Summer temperatures are usually between −7° and 21°C (19 to 70°F). But summer air can reach 30°C (86°F) with very high humidity. Taiga's cooler temperatures reduce evaporation. That is why taiga biomes are wetter than grasslands. It helps preserve taiga's wetlands, ponds, lakes, bogs, and mossy forest floor.

Taiga soil is shallow and acidic. Low temperatures reduce the rate of decomposition. As a result, the forest floor has a lot of slowly decaying or undecayed plant matter. There are also herbs, mushrooms, lichens, and mosses. Where sunlight reaches the forest floor, you might find blueberries in the summer, baby willows, alders, and fungi.

"Coniferous forest" describes the biome quite well. Most trees are conifers—spruce, pines, fir, and tamarack. But there are also broad-leafed trees—birch, alder, poplar, balsam, aspen—particularly along a taiga biome's southern border. In Siberia, tamarack, which sheds its leaves in autumn, is the dominant species.

Sometimes the North American taiga is called the spruce-moose forest! This is because it has an abundance of spruce trees and moose. But there are other animals—bear, beavers, martens, mink, lynx, foxes, wolves, wolverines, muskrats, arctic hares, squirrels, voles, and weasels. In the winter, only thirty bird species brave the cold. Among them are gray owls, ptarmigans, and whooping cranes. In the summer, millions of birds (more than three hundred species) from as far away as the tropics migrate to the taiga to nest and breed. They are drawn there by an abundance of insects. Those insects include flies, mosquitoes, beetles, larch sawflies, spruce budworms, and other bugs. The swarms of insects can send hikers searching for shelter. Because of the temperature, few cold-blooded animals, other than insects, can be found in the taiga. Insect eggs can survive the winter and hatch when warm weather arrives. Reptiles and amphibians can't endure the cold, but fish are common in the biome's lakes and rivers.

Migrating animals, other than birds, include butterflies, salmon, and caribou. Caribou spend the winter in the taiga and the summer in the colder tundra to the north.

Moose make their home in the taiga.

Not a lot of snow falls in the winter, but it is cold all season and sunlight is limited. As a result, snow doesn't melt. It accumulates and deepens. Some animals, such as voles, weasels, and hares, make tunnels under the snow. A foot under the snow's surface, the temperature is a relatively toasty 0°C (32°F). The deep snow insulates these animals from the much colder air above. The insulation, their furry bodies, and the food they store underground keep them warm.

Large animals with long legs, such as moose, can walk through the snow. Others, such as lynx and arctic hares, have broad paws. Their broad paws act like snowshoes, allowing them to walk on top of the deep snow.

The Scientific Method

To do experiments the way scientists do, you need to know about the scientific method. It is true that scientists in different areas of science use different ways of experimenting. Depending on the problem, one method is likely to be better than another. Designing a new medicine for heart disease and finding

These migrating caribou are in Alaska during the fall.

evidence of water on Mars require different kinds of experiments.

Despite these differences, all scientists use a similar approach as they experiment. It is called the scientific method. In most experimenting, some or all of the following steps are used: making an observation, coming up with a question, creating a hypothesis (a possible answer to the question) and a prediction (an if-then statement), designing and conducting an experiment, analyzing results, drawing conclusions about the prediction, and deciding if the hypothesis is true or false. Scientists share the results of their experiments by writing articles that are published in science journals.

You might wonder how to use the scientific method. You begin when you see, read, or hear about something in the world that makes you curious. So you ask a question. To find an answer, you do a well-designed investigation; you use the scientific method.

Once you have a question, you can make a hypothesis. Your hypothesis is a possible answer to the question (what you think is true). For example, you might hypothesize that rainfall in all forest biomes—taiga, temperate, and rain forest—is approximately the same. Once you have a hypothesis, it is time to design an experiment to test your hypothesis.

In most cases, you should do a controlled experiment. This means having two subjects that are treated the same except for the one thing being tested. That thing is called a variable. To test the hypothesis above, you might measure the annual rainfall (the variable) in all forest biomes for a decade. You would find that the rainfall in a taiga biome is less than in either temperate forests or rain forests. You would have to conclude that your hypothesis was not correct.

The results of one experiment often lead to another question. In the case above, that experiment might lead you to wonder what effect less rainfall has on the kind of plants and animals we find in different forests. Whatever the results, something can be learned from every experiment!

Science Fairs

Some of the investigations in this book contain ideas that might be used as a science fair project. Those ideas are indicated with a symbol ( ). However, judges at science fairs do not reward projects or experiments that are simply copied from a book. For example, diagrams of leaves from conifers and deciduous trees would not impress most judges. However, an experiment that measured the effect of rainfall on the growth rate of different conifer species would probably attract their attention.

Science fair judges tend to reward creative thought and imagination. It is difficult to be creative or imaginative unless you are really interested in your project. Therefore, try to choose something that excites you. And before you jump into a project, consider, too, your own talents and the cost of the materials you will need.

If you decide to use an experiment or idea found in this book as a science fair project, find ways to modify or extend it. This should not be difficult. As you do investigations, new ideas will come to mind. You will think of questions that experiments can answer. The experiments will make excellent science fair projects, especially because the ideas are yours and are interesting to you.

Safety First

Safety is very important in science. Certain rules should be followed when doing experiments. Some of the rules below may seem obvious to you, others may not, but it is important that you follow all of them.

1. Do any experiments or projects, whether from this book or of your own design, **under the adult supervision** of a science teacher or other knowledgeable adult.

2. Read all instructions carefully before proceeding with a project. If you have questions, check with your supervisor before going further.

3. **Always wear safety goggles** when doing experiments that could cause particles to enter your eyes. Tie back long hair and do not wear open-toed shoes.

4. Do not eat or drink while experimenting. Never taste substances being used (unless instructed to do so).

5. Do not touch chemicals with bare hands.

6. Do not let water drops fall on a hot lightbulb.

7. The liquid in some older thermometers is mercury (a dense liquid metal). It is dangerous to touch mercury or breathe its vapor. That is why mercury thermometers have been banned in many states. When doing experiments, use only nonmercury thermometers, such as digital thermometers or those filled with alcohol. If you have a mercury thermometer in the house, **ask an adult** to take it to a place where it can be exchanged or safely discarded.

8. Do only those experiments that are described in the book or those that have been approved **by an adult**.

9. Maintain a serious attitude while conducting experiments. Never engage in horseplay or play practical jokes.

10. Remove all items not needed for the experiment from your work space.

11. At the end of every activity, clean all materials used and put them away. Then wash your hands thoroughly with soap and water.

A Note About Your Notebook

Your notebook, as any scientist will tell you, is a valuable possession. It should contain ideas you may have as you experiment, sketches you draw, calculations you make, and hypotheses you suggest. It should include a description of every experiment you do and the data you record, such as volumes, temperatures, masses, and so on. It should also contain the results of your experiments, graphs you draw, and any conclusions you make based on your results.

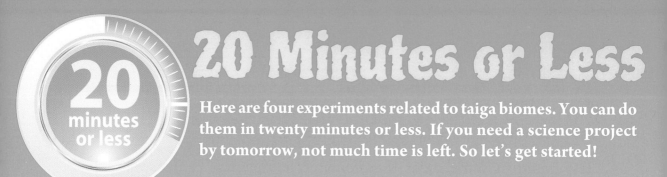

20 Minutes or Less

20 minutes or less

Here are four experiments related to taiga biomes. You can do them in twenty minutes or less. If you need a science project by tomorrow, not much time is left. So let's get started!

1. Using Maps (20 minutes)

What's the Plan?

Let's find out where taiga biomes are located around the world. And let's find out in which type of biome you live.

WHAT YOU NEED:

- **map of biomes in Figure 1**
- **map of the world or large world globe**

What You Do

1. Examine the map in Figure 1. It shows where taiga and other biomes are located.

2. Look at the places where taiga biomes are found. Compare them with the same places on a map of the world or on a world globe.

3. On which continents do you find taiga biomes? Are there any continents that do not have a taiga biome?

4. Find where you live on a world map. Then, using Figure 1, find the biome in which you live.

What's Going On?

When you compared the map of biomes in Figure 1 with a map of the world, you could see that taiga biomes are not found in Africa, Australia, South America, or Antarctica. They exist only in the Northern Hemisphere.

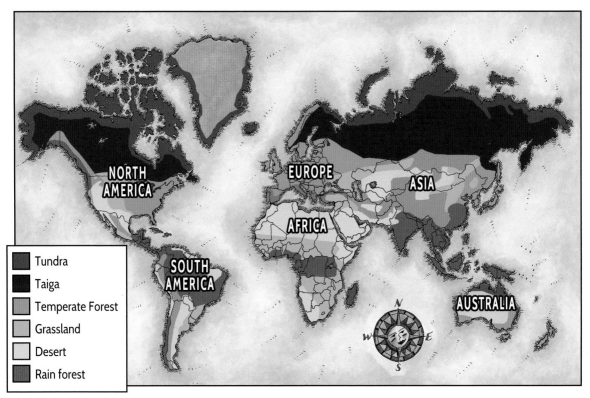

Figure 1. The world's land biomes

Legend:
- Tundra
- Taiga
- Temperate Forest
- Grassland
- Desert
- Rain forest

By a similar comparison, you could see in which type of biome you live. Don't be surprised if you think the biome map for your home is wrong. The map shows what is true for much of the region where you live, not every part of it. For example, the author lives on Cape Cod in Massachusetts. The biome map indicates that he lives in a temperate forest biome. However, the outer end of Cape Cod is covered by sand dunes. Also, while forest covers much of Cape Cod, the trees are shorter than in a typical temperate forest. This is caused by the strong winds and salt air coming off the Atlantic Ocean.

2. A Climatogram of a City in a Taiga Biome
(20 minutes)

WHAT YOU NEED:
- **graph paper**
- **pen or pencil**

What's the Plan?

Let's make a climatogram for Anchorage, Alaska. It is within a taiga biome.

What You Do

1. Figure 2 shows what a climatogram looks like. Months of the year are plotted along the horizontal axis. Rainfall is plotted along the left vertical axis, temperature along the right vertical axis.

   Use a sheet of graph paper to make a climatogram for Anchorage. The climatogram will show Anchorage's average monthly temperature and rainfall. The data in Table 1 has the information you need. Use it to make a climatogram for Anchorage, Alaska.

Table 1: Monthly average temperatures and precipitation for Anchorage, Alaska												
	Jan.	Feb.	Mar.	Apr.	May	Jun.	Jul.	Aug.	Sept.	Oct.	Nov.	Dec.
Temp. (°C)	-10.3	-8.2	-4.2	1.8	8.5	12.2	14.6	13.5	9.1	0.7	-6.8	-9.5
Precip (in)	0.3	0.2	2.5	0.3	0.7	1.3	0.6	0.6	1.6	1.9	2.8	2.3

2. What is the approximate average temperature for one year in Anchorage?

3. What is the approximate total average rainfall for one year in Anchorage?

4. Are Anchorage's temperatures and rainfall normal for a taiga biome? Does Anchorage have cool summers and cold winters? Does it have 12 to 33 inches of precipitation?

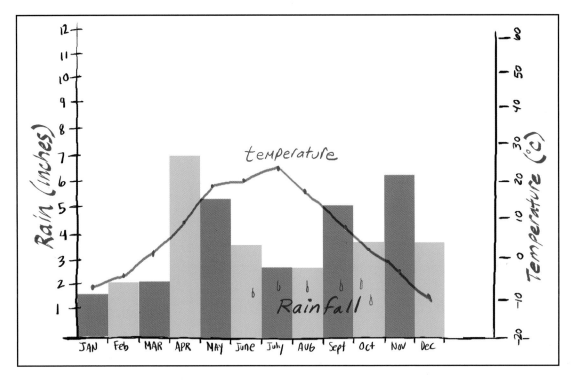

Figure 2. This is a sample climatogram. Now it is your turn to make one for Anchorage, Alaska.

What's Going On?

Your climatogram should show Anchorage's average monthly temperature and rainfall in a graphical way. The approximate total annual precipitation in Anchorage is 15.1 inches. The approximate average annual temperature is 1.8°C (35.2°F). These numbers are normal for a taiga biome.

Keep Exploring–If You Have More Time!

- Prepare a climatogram of your city or town. What is your total yearly precipitation? Do you have cold winters and warm summers? What is your average annual temperature?

3. A Taiga Animal's Wide Feet and Pressure (20 minutes)

WHAT YOU NEED:
- **soft clay or play dough (Play–Doh™)**
- **ruler**
- **short wood dowels, one wide, one narrow, or a narrow pill bottle and an unsharpened pencil**
- **partner**
- **weight, such as a book or books**

What's the Plan?

Some animals that live in a taiga biome, such as the lynx and arctic hare, have wide feet. Let's see how that feature helps keep them from sinking deep into the winter snow.

What You Do

1. Find some soft clay or play dough (Play-Doh™). Make a layer of clay that is several centimeters thick.

2. Put a narrow, short dowel or a thick, unsharpened pencil on the clay. Guide the dowel while a partner places a weight of some kind on the top of the dowel. Let the weight rest on top of the dowel or pencil. The dowel will be pressed into the clay (Figure 3a).

3. Repeat the experiment with a short, wide, wood dowel or a narrow pill bottle. Use the same weight (Figure 3b).

   Compare the two impressions that were made in the clay. What do you conclude? What does this experiment have to do with animals walking on snow?

An arctic hare has wide feet. How does that help it in the snow?

Figure 3. How far do these dowels sink into the clay when an equal weight pushes on each?

What's Going On?

The impression made by the narrow dowel or pencil was deeper than the one made by the wider dowel. This shows why an animal with wide feet will not sink as deeply into snow as the same animal with smaller feet. What you saw was a difference in pressure. The force (weight) on both wide and narrow dowels was the same. But the area on which the weight acted was different. The area pushing on the clay was greater for the wide dowel. Pressure (P) is equal to the force (F) divided by the area (A) on which the force acts (P = F/A). The pressure was less when the force acted on the wider dowel. Therefore, it did not sink as far into the clay as did the narrower dowel. The same is true for the wide feet of some taiga animals.

Keep Exploring–If You Have More Time!

• Design and do an experiment to show that air exerts a pressure.

17

4. Seasons in a Taiga (20 minutes)

What's the Plan?

Let's do an experiment to see why taiga biomes have seasons.

WHAT YOU NEED:

- sheet of paper
- table
- dark room
- large protractor
- flashlight

What You Do

Anchorage, the largest city in Alaska, lies within North America's taiga biome. Its latitude is slightly more than 61 degrees north. At the beginning of summer (June 21), the midday sun at this latitude reaches an altitude of approximately 52 degrees. At the beginning of winter (December 21), the midday sun is only about six degrees above the horizon. As you might guess, daylight in Anchorage in late December is very limited.

1. Place a sheet of paper on a table. Turn off lights or close shades to make the room dark.

2. Hold a large protractor upright on the paper.

3. Let a flashlight represent the sun. Shine the light onto the paper at an angle of about 52 degrees (Figure 4a). Notice the light on the paper. The paper represents taiga land at about 60 degrees latitude.

4. Move the flashlight so that it strikes the paper at an angle of about six degrees. Again, notice the light that shines on the paper. What can you conclude?

What's Going On?

As you saw, winter sunlight on a taiga biome is far less intense than summer sunlight. The winter sun's light is more spread out. The sunlight, shining

18

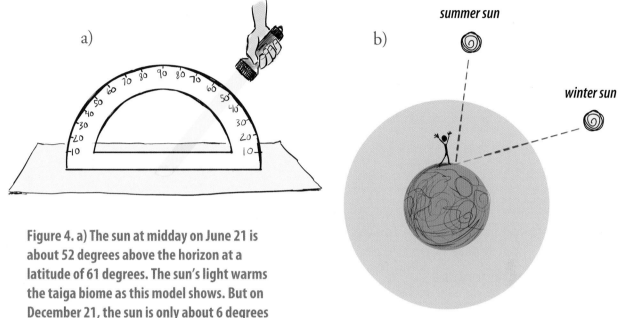

Figure 4. a) The sun at midday on June 21 is about 52 degrees above the horizon at a latitude of 61 degrees. The sun's light warms the taiga biome as this model shows. But on December 21, the sun is only about 6 degrees above the horizon at midday. Then the light is much less intense and shines for only a short time. b) Winter sunlight has a longer path through Earth's atmosphere. So more of its energy is absorbed before it reaches the ground.

at six degrees, covers a much larger area than at 52 degrees. This makes the winter sunlight far less intense. The more direct summer sunlight provides greater warmth to the biome. During winter, the less intense light leads to low air temperatures. The result of the sun's different angles helps explain taiga seasons. And, too, the winter sun passes through more atmosphere where some of its energy is absorbed (Figure 4b). Furthermore, the winter sun is above the horizon for much less time.

Keep Exploring–If You Have More Time!

- Design and do an experiment to measure the altitude of the midday sun at the latitude where you live. Repeat the experiment at the beginning of each season.

- Does midday always occur at the same time? Do experiments to find out.

30 Minutes or Less

These two experiments take about thirty minutes. They are worth every minute!

5. Soil Acidity (30 minutes)

What's the Plan?

Taiga soil is acidic. This means its pH (a measure of acidity) is less than 7. Let's measure the pH of soil near your home.

What You Do

Soils may be acidic, alkaline (basic), or neutral. Acids form hydrogen ions (H+) in water. Hydrogen ions are hydrogen atoms that have lost an electron. An acid's strength depends on its concentration of hydrogen ions. pH is a measure of hydrogen ion concentration. Substances with a pH less than 7 are acidic; substances with a pH greater than 7 are basic (alkaline); substances with a pH of 7 are neutral. Very acidic soil has a pH of 3 to 5. Soils with a pH of 8 to 10 are very basic. Most plants don't do well in soils with a pH greater than 8.

Paper pH strips can be used to measure the entire pH range from 1 to 14.

1. To find the pH of soil in your garden, flower bed, or lawn, fill a jar about one-third of the way with soil. Add water until the jar is about two-thirds full.

WHAT YOU NEED:

- soil from a garden, flower bed, or lawn
- plastic jar with lid
- water
- tweezers
- pH paper strips with a chart showing the paper's color at different pH values

2. Put a cover on the jar. Shake it vigorously to mix the soil and water thoroughly.

3. Let the soil settle for five minutes.

4. Use tweezers to hold the end of a pH paper strip. Dip the other end into the soil solution. Remove the strip and compare the color of the wet pH paper with the color chart provided with the strips. What is the pH of the soil you tested?

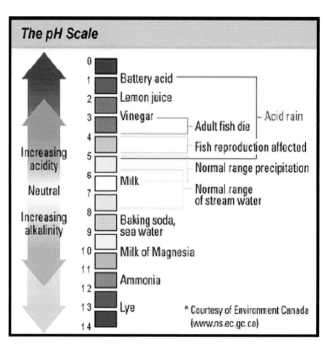

This pH scale shows the range of pH for items, from strong battery acid to very basic lye.

What's Going On?

The pH paper's color revealed the pH of the soil you tested. How does it compare with the pH of acidic taiga soil?

Keep Exploring–If You Have More Time!

- Vinegar is acidic and ammonia water is basic. Add drops of grape juice (unsweetened) to vinegar and to ammonia water to see whether it can be used to identify acids and bases.

6. How Permafrost Helps Keep a Taiga Wet
(30 minutes)

WHAT YOU NEED:
- dry sand
- 3 plastic vials (30 to 50 mL volume)
- water
- eyedropper
- freezer
- food coloring

What's the Plan?

Northern taiga biomes may have permafrost beneath the top layer of soil. Permafrost is permanently frozen soil. Let's see how permafrost helps keep a taiga biome wet.

What You Do

1. Add dry sand to a plastic vial until it is about a third full. The sand represents taiga soil.

2. Slowly add water to the sand. When the spaces between the sand grains are filled with water, stop. If there is water above the sand, remove it with an eyedropper. Place the vial in a freezer. When frozen, it will be your "permafrost." See Figure 5a.

3. Add a drop of food coloring to a second vial. Fill the vial with water.

4. Add dry sand to a third plastic vial. Add sand until the vial is about one-third full.

5. Add the colored water to the dry sand in the third vial until it is about two-thirds full (Figure 5b). Watch the colored water move down through the sand.

6. When your "permafrost" is thoroughly frozen, pour dry sand onto the "permafrost." Add sand until the vial is about two-thirds full. Slowly add colored water to the sand. What happens when the water reaches the permafrost (Figure 5c)?

22

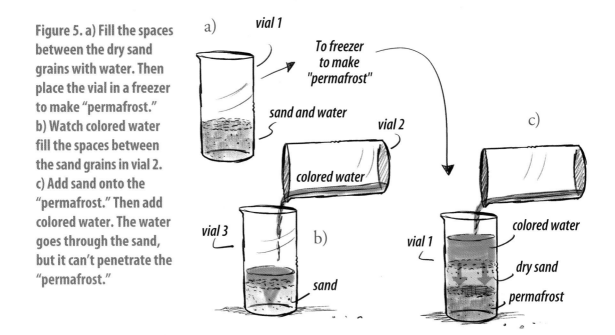

Figure 5. a) Fill the spaces between the dry sand grains with water. Then place the vial in a freezer to make "permafrost." b) Watch colored water fill the spaces between the sand grains in vial 2. c) Add sand onto the "permafrost." Then add colored water. The water goes through the sand, but it can't penetrate the "permafrost."

What's Going On?

As you saw in step 6, when the colored water reached the "permafrost," it stopped. It could not move into the permafrost. It's similar to a frozen pond. In the summer, you can jump into the water. But if it's frozen in the winter, you can't reach the water.

Normally, water can move deep down into the soil. Permafrost prevents water from draining deep into soil. As a result, more water collects on or near the top of the soil. This keeps the ground wet or damp. It also prevents water in bogs and ponds from draining into the ground.

Keep Exploring–If You Have More Time!

• Design and do an experiment to determine what fraction of dry sand is actually air.

One Hour or Less

1 hour or less

The next six experiments can be done in about one hour or less.

7. Taiga Snow in Sun and Shade (1 hour)

What's the Plan?

Let's see if we can understand why a taiga biome has so much snow in the winter. We know it does not receive a huge amount of snow. Yet its forests often contain deep snow.

What You Do

1. Find two small, identical aluminum pans. Label them "1" and "2."

2. Weigh and record the masses of the two small pans. They should be very nearly the same.

3. Use another container to collect some loose snow.

4. Add equal masses of snow to the two small pans.

5. Place one pan in the sun near a window. Tip the pan by sliding something under one side. The sun should shine directly on the snow. Place the other pan nearby in the shade (Figure 6).

    In which pan does the snow melt faster?

WHAT YOU NEED:

- **2 small, identical, shallow aluminum pans**
- **larger container**
- **marking pen**
- **balance that can weigh to ± 0.1 g**
- **pen or pencil**
- **notebook**
- **loose snow**
- **bright sun**
- **shade**

What's Going On?

You probably found the snow melted faster in the sun than in the shade. A taiga biome has lots of conifer trees. Therefore, there is plenty of shade in a taiga forest. The shade helps prevent the snow from melting. Other factors that help preserve the snow include cold temperatures, limited sun, and limited rain.

Keep Exploring—If You Have More Time!

- During the winter, look for places that are shaded all day. Look too for places that receive lots of sun. What do your observations tell you?

- This house is located in the state of Connecticut. The photograph, which shows some lingering snow, was taken after an early spring thaw. On which side of the house do you think this snow was located? (Answer on p. 47.)

window

snow in the shade

snow in the sunlight

Figure 6. Two equal masses of snow are placed so that one is in bright sunlight and the other is in shade.

This photo shows some snow outside a house in Connecticut.

8. Animal Tracks (1 hour)

What's the Plan?

During a taiga winter, animals leave footprints (tracks) in the snow. Let's try to identify tracks that you may find in the snow or dirt near your home.

What You Do

1. Look for tracks around your home. The best time to find them is after a light snow. Animal tracks show up well in snow. They are also easy to see in moist dirt or in mud. Dog and cat tracks are the most common (Figure 7). Can you find any cat or dog tracks? Can you identify which are cat tracks and which are dog tracks?

2. Tracks made by wild animals are less common than those made by dogs or cats. The tracks of some common wild animals are also seen in Figure 7. Can you find any wild animal tracks in snow or dirt near your home? If you find some, try to identify the animals that made them.

3. Of course, humans also make tracks. Can you find human tracks? Were they made by a child or an adult? If an adult, were they made by a man or a woman? How can you tell?

4. Make a permanent record of the tracks you find by photographing them.

What's Going On?

You can probably find tracks around your home. Use Figure 7 to identify the common ones you find. To identify tracks of less common wild animals, go to the Internet. Or look for a book on, or a guide to, animal tracks.

Adult tracks are larger and farther apart than children's tracks. Men's tracks are usually longer and wider than women's tracks.

squirrel

cat

dog

rabbit

deer

(front)

pigeon

sparrow

woodpecker

(back)

bird tracks

raccoon

Figure 7. These are some common nonhuman tracks you may find near your home.

Keep Exploring–If You Have More Time!

- What other tracks can you find? Can you identify a car by its tire tracks? Can you distinguish truck tracks from car tracks? On a farm, can you identify tractor tracks? Cow tracks? Horse tracks? Other animal tracks?

9. Making Casts of Tracks in Snow or Dirt (1 hour)

WHAT YOU NEED:
- **well formed tracks**
- **plaster of Paris**
- **water**
- **small pan to hold plaster**
- **scissors**
- **manila folder**
- **paper clips**
- **clock or watch**
- **a dull knife**
- **snow**

What's the Plan?

During a taiga winter, animals leave footprints in the snow. In the summer, they leave tracks in moist soil. Let's preserve some animal and other tracks by making casts of them.

What You Do

1. Find a deep, well formed track in soil. It's the best kind to preserve in a cast.

2. Mix plaster of Paris in a small pan with water. The mixture should feel like thick pancake batter.

3. Cut a long, one-inch-wide strip from a manila folder. Use paper clips to make it into a loop. Insert the collar you have made around the track (Figure 8a).

4. Pour the plaster of Paris slowly into the track until it almost reaches the top of the collar (Figure 8b).

5. Wait about 20 minutes for the plaster to harden. Then dig around the cast with a dull knife.

6. Remove the cast. Wash the mud and dirt off the bottom of the cast.

7. Making casts of tracks made in snow is more difficult. But it can be done in cold weather. Add some snow to the plaster to make it colder. Before pouring the plaster onto the track, sprinkle a little water onto the track.

a)

b)

Figure 8. a) Surround the track with a collar. b) Pour plaster of Paris onto the track.

This will form a thin layer of ice over the track, making it harder. Slowly pour the plaster onto the track and proceed as before.

What's Going On?

When the plaster of Paris hardens, a raised print of the track will have been preserved.

Keep Exploring–If You Have More Time!

- Make a collection of track casts. Make casts for a variety of animals.

10. The Melting Point of Snow (1 hour)

WHAT YOU NEED:

- **cold winter day when there is lots of snow**
- **pail**
- **quart container**
- **foam coffee cup**
- **thermometer (–10– 50°C or 0–120°F)**

What's the Plan?

In the winter, taiga forests are covered with snow. Let's find the air temperature that is needed for the snow to melt.

What You Do

1. On a cold winter day when there is lots of snow on the ground, go outside. Bring inside a pailful, a quart, and a cup of snow from outside.

2. Quickly place a thermometer in the cup of snow. Stir the snow as it begins to melt. Watch the thermometer as the temperature decreases. At what temperature does it stop decreasing?

3. Repeat the experiment with the quart of snow. What is the melting temperature of this larger amount of snow?

4. Repeat the experiment with the pailful of snow. What is the melting temperature of this larger amount of snow? Does the melting temperature depend on the mass of snow?

What's Going On?

You probably found the temperature in all three containers fell to about 0 degrees Celsius or 32 degrees Fahrenheit and remained there as the snow melted. The mass (amount) of the snow did not affect the melting temperature. Melting points are independent of mass.

You also saw that the snow melted quite slowly. Snow in a taiga forest may last well into the spring before all of it has melted.

Joseph Black, an eighteenth-century Scottish scientist, measured the heat to melt snow. He once wrote, "Were the ice and snow to melt suddenly . . . the torrents and inundations would be . . . irresistible and dreadful. They would tear up and sweep away everything."

Keep Exploring–If You Have More Time!

- Design and do an experiment to find out how much heat is needed to melt a gram of snow. (Because snow consists of tiny crystals of ice [snowflakes], you might find it easier to melt an ice cube rather than snow.)

11. How Cool Temperatures Help Keep a Taiga Wet
(1 hour)

WHAT YOU NEED:

- paper towels
- sink
- cold water faucet
- a balance that can weigh to ±1 gram
- pen or pencil
- notebook
- cool place
- warm room
- clock or watch

What's the Plan?

A taiga biome receives about the same amount of rain as a grassland. But although a grassland is generally dry, a taiga is usually damp or wet. Let's find out why a taiga biome might be wetter than grassland.

What You'll Do

1. Wet two folded paper towels in a sink. Hold them under a running cold water faucet.

2. Open the towels. Let any excess water drain away into the sink.

3. Fold both towels again. Then weigh each towel on a balance that can weigh to ±1 gram. Record the weight of each towel in your notebook.

4. Fully open both towels. Hang one on a line in cool (not freezing) air, perhaps in a cool garage or basement.

5. Hang the other towel in a room with warm air, such as in a kitchen.

6. After one hour, reweigh each towel and record its weight. From which towel did more water evaporate?

What's Going On?

You probably found that more water evaporated from the towel that was in warm air. The cool temperatures found in a taiga biome reduce the rate at which water evaporates. That is one reason why soil, plants, puddles, bogs, and all things in a taiga are usually wetter than in a grassland.

Keep Exploring–If You Have More Time!

- Grasslands are open land with relatively few trees. Taiga is a biome with lots of trees. For that reason, much of a taiga biome is shaded and protected from wind. Design and do an experiment to show that shade also reduces the rate at which water evaporates.

12. How Many Board Feet in That Tree? (1 hour)

WHAT YOU NEED:

• partner

• tall pine tree

• tape measure

• calculator (optional)

What's the Plan?

A taiga biome is often called a coniferous forest because the predominate trees in the biome are conifers—spruce, pines, fir, and tamarack. Conifers are a source of lumber. So taiga biomes attract lumber companies. Like foresters hired by lumber companies, you can estimate the number of board feet in a tall pine tree. Lumber is measured in board feet. A board foot is one square foot of wood with a thickness of one inch (Figure 9a). Before we can find the number of board feet, we need to estimate the volume of wood in the tree's trunk. (Branches are usually discarded unless they are very large and straight.)

What You Do

1. Begin by estimating the volume of wood in a tree trunk. To do this, ask a partner to stand next to a tall pine tree. You should stand about 60 to 70 feet from the tree.

2. Hold your hand at arm's length in front of you. Separate your thumb and finger until they match your friend's height as seen from where you stand.

3. Find out how many of your partner's heights equal the tree's height. You can do that by moving your separated thumb and finger upward one partner height at a time (Figure 9b). Count the number of partner heights that match the tree's height.

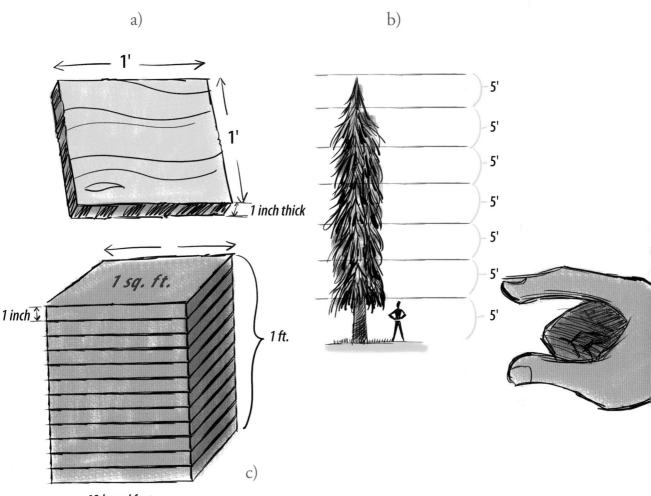

a)

b)

1'

1'

1 inch thick

1 sq. ft.

1 inch

1 ft.

12 board feet

5'

5'

5'

5'

5'

5'

5'

c)

Figure 9. a) A board foot is a square foot of wood that is one inch thick. b) Estimating the height of a tree: The one shown is about seven partner heights. c) The drawing shows that a cubic foot of lumber contains 12 board feet. Each board foot is one inch thick.

4. Knowing your partner's height, estimate the tree's height. For example, suppose your partner is five feet tall and the tree is ten times taller than your partner. Then the estimated height of the tree would be 50 feet.

5. Now you can start estimating the volume of wood in the tree's trunk. Using a tape measure, find the tree's trunk circumference at the base of the tree.

6. Assume the tree's trunk circumference decreases uniformly from base to tree top. Think of it as a long, thin cone. The volume of a cone is $1/3\ \pi r^2 h$. The radius, r, is the radius of the cone's circular base, and h is the cone's height. Using your measurements and assumptions, find the number of board feet in the tree.

What's Going On?

Suppose the tree is 50 feet tall and the circumference of its base is 3.14 feet. A cone with a circumference of 3.14 feet and a height of 50 feet has a volume given by the formula for a cone's volume—$1/3\ \pi r^2 h$. For this tree, the volume of wood available for lumber would be equal to $1/3\ \pi \times (0.5\ \text{ft})^2 \times 50\ \text{ft} = 13\ \text{ft}^3$. (Remember, the diameter of a circle equals its circumference divided by π, and its radius is half the diameter.) In this case, the radius is half a foot or six inches.

To find the number of board feet, you simply multiply the volume by 12, because a cubic foot of wood contains 12 board feet. Figure 9c shows you why there are 12 board feet in a cubic foot of wood.

Keep Exploring–If You Have More Time!

• Find a way to show that the volume of a cone is $1/3\ \pi r^2 h$ or one-third the volume of a cylinder, which is $\pi r^2 h$, the area of the cylinder's base times its height.

- Unless lumber is to be utilized for building log cabins, the tree's bark is not used to make boards. How would you take the unused bark into account when estimating the board feet in a tree?

- How could you use a tree's shadow to measure its height?

- Measure the trunk's base circumference and height for a number of pine trees. Can you make a good estimate of the height of a tree by knowing the base diameter of its trunk?

- Do an experiment to determine the density of pine wood. Then estimate the mass of the tree trunk that you measured in Experiment 12.

1 hour or more

More Than One Hour

The remaining experiments take longer. But if you are a budding scientist, you will find they are worth the time!

13. Snow as an Insulator
(4 hours; 2 hours per experiment)

WHAT YOU NEED:

- 2 small plastic containers, with covers, having a volume of about 100 mL (large pill containers from drugstores work well)
- large nail to make holes in the center of the covers so lab thermometers can be inserted into the containers
- warm water
- graduated cylinder or metric measuring cup
- 2 thermometers (–10 to 50°C or –20 to 120°F)
- 2 large plastic containers
- snow
- freezer
- clock or watch
- pen or pencil
- notebook
- graph paper
- 3 identical ice cubes
- 3 small, clear, plastic bags
- twisties
- 2 large plastic cups
- 2 (foam) coffee cups

What's the Plan?

Taiga winters are very cold, so snow accumulates on the forest floor. Many animals burrow deep into the snow to stay warm. The snow insulates them from the much colder air temperatures above the snow. Let's see if snow really acts as an insulator. First, we'll experiment with outgoing heat. Then we'll experiment with incoming heat.

What You Do

1. Add about 70 mL of lukewarm water to two small plastic containers. Place covers on the containers and use a nail to make a hole in each cover. Insert a thermometer through each cover. The bulb should be near the middle of the water in each container (Figure 10a). Put one small container in one of the larger plastic containers.

2. Add snow to the bottom of the other larger container. Put the other small container on the snow. Then surround the sides and top of the small container with snow (Figure 10b).

3. Put both large containers and their contents into a freezer. Record the water temperature in each container initially and at ten-minute intervals. When water in the containers reaches 0°C (32°F) or the temperature stops decreasing, remove them from the freezer. The water has started to freeze.

4. Use your data to plot temperature versus time for both containers. Do both plots on the same graph. (See Figure 10c). What evidence do you have to indicate that snow is an insulator?

What's Going On?

Your graphs probably show that the temperature changed more slowly in the container surrounded by snow than in the one resting in air. This indicates that heat is moving out of the snow-insulated water more slowly than it is from water in the other container.

Now let's see if the same is true when heat moves into something.

What You Do

1. Place three identical ice cubes in small, clear, plastic bags. Squeeze the bags to remove any air around the ice. Then seal the bags with twisties.

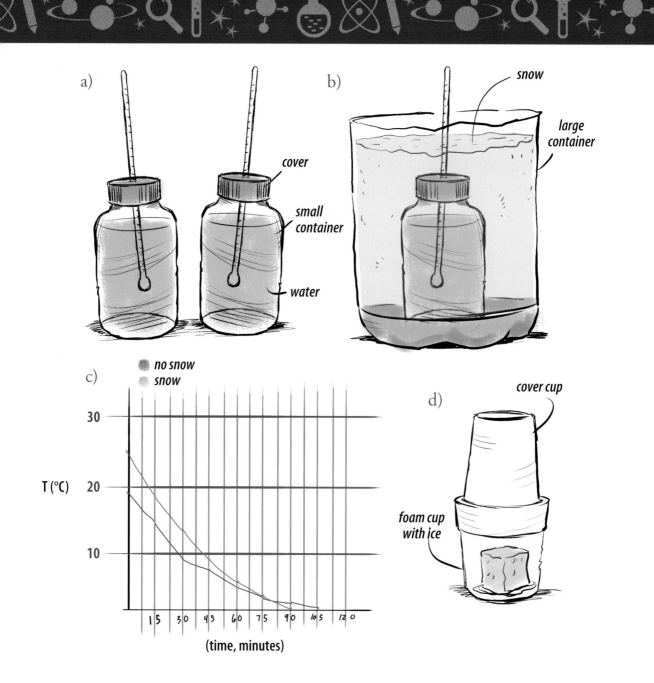

Figure 10. a) Two small containers are equipped with water and thermometers. b) One small container is placed in a larger container and surrounded with snow. c) This graph shows the data collected by the author when he measured water temperatures over a two-hour period for the two containers, one of which was covered with snow . d) Cup 2, containing the ice, is covered by a second foam cup.

2. Place one ice cube in a plastic cup (cup 1). Place another in an insulated (foam) coffee cup (cup 2). Cover it with a second foam cup that has its upper third cut off (Figure 10d). Put snow in the bottom half of another plastic cup (cup 3). Put the third ice cube on the snow. Then add more snow to surround the ice and fill the rest of the cup.

3. Leave the three cups on a counter at room temperature. When snow in cup 3 begins to melt, remove it. Replace with fresh snow.

4. Check the cubes and snow every few minutes until the ice cube in cup 1 has completely melted. How big is the ice cube in cup 2? How big is the ice cube in cup 3?

What's Going On?

As you have probably seen, snow kept the ice cube in cup 3 from melting as quickly as the ice in cup 1. Some ice may also have remained in cup 3 after the ice in cup 2 melted.

These experiments show that snow is an insulator. Snow slows the movement of heat out of warm matter (the water in the first experiment). And it slows the movement of heat into a cold substance (the ice in the second experiment).

Keep Exploring–If You Have More Time!

- Will ice melt faster in warm air or cold air? In warm water or cold water? Do experiments to find out.
- If you place ice cubes in water, does the time to melt the ice depend on the volume of water? Do an experiment to find out.
- If the volume of several pieces of ice is the same, does the shape of the ice affect the time for them to melt? How can you find out?
- If they have the same volume, which will melt faster, a cube of ice or a pancake-shaped piece of ice?

14. The Sun's Heat in a Taiga Biome (1 Day)

What's the Plan?

Anchorage is in North America's taiga biome. It is at about 61 degrees north latitude. During the summer, the midday sun reaches an altitude as high as 52 degrees. But in winter, the midday sun is only about six degrees above the horizon. What effect does the sun's altitude have on the solar energy it provides? Let's absorb solar energy at midday when the sun is highest and near sunset or sunrise when it is low in the sky.

WHAT YOU NEED:

- bright sunny day
- graduated cylinder or metric measuring cup
- water
- black ink
- eye dropper
- thermometer
- clear plastic container that holds slightly more than 100 mL
- notebook
- pen or pencil
- south-facing and west-facing windows
- clock or watch

What You Do

1. Around midday, add a few drops of black ink to a clear plastic container that should hold at least 100 mL of water. (Black water will absorb more solar energy than clear water.)

2. Add 100 mL of water at or slightly below room temperature to the container.

3. Stir with a thermometer and record the temperature of the water.

4. Place the water in bright sunlight near a south-facing window (Figure 11).

5. After 30 minutes, stir the water with the thermometer and record the temperature.

The midday winter sun is low on the horizon during winter and casts long shadows.

6. Repeat the experiment about an hour before sunset when the sun is low in the sky. This time, place the water near a west-facing window.

What can you conclude from these two experiments?

What's Going On?

You probably found that the temperature change of the water was greater near midday than near sunset. The reason is that the higher midday sun caused more solar energy to enter the water than did the lower late-day sun. The sun provides Earth with more energy the greater its altitude above the horizon.

Keep Exploring–If You Have More Time!

- How much heat, in calories, was transmitted to the water at midday and near sunset?

- By how much did black ink increase the absorption of solar energy?

15. What Do Owls Eat?
(Several Days)

WHAT YOU NEED:

- **owl pellets (regurgitated prey owls have eaten)**
- **bag**
- **gloves**
- **newspapers**
- **tweezers**

What's the Plan?

Owls are one of the few birds that inhabit a taiga biome all year. You can discover what owls eat by dissecting the pellets they regurgitate.

What You Do

1. Look for owl pellets. Owl pellets can be found beneath trees where owls roost. The pellets are about two to three inches long and one to one and a half inches wide. They are dark gray in color and contain the skeletal remains of the prey that was eaten. Owls do not have teeth. They swallow their prey whole and regurgitate the hair and bones that are not digested in their stomachs.

2. Gather a few owl pellets. They might be found in a barn, beneath trees in the woods, in a cemetery, under palm trees, even in a church steeple. Often, a farmer will tell you of owls he has heard on his property and will allow

This burrowing owl is expelling a pellet.

you to search for pellets. Pellets can also be purchased from a science supply house.

3. Although owl pellets are usually safe to touch, play it safe and wear gloves. Pick up several pellets and place them in a bag.

These opened barn owl pellets show the rodent bones.

4. Back home, place the pellets on newspapers. Use tweezers to pick away hair from the skulls and other bones in the pellets. Can you identify the animals the owl ate? Try to identify any of the bones you find, such as leg bones (tibia, fibula, femur, ulna), ribs, etc.

What's Going On?

Owls do not have teeth, so they can't chew food. Their hooked beaks can rip and tear their prey, but the unchewed remains are swallowed. In the owl's stomach, the flesh is digested by acids and enzymes. The undigested hair and bones are later regurgitated in the form of pellets. You probably were able to identify one or more skulls, leg bones, and ribs. You could tell they were from small animals, such as mice and voles.

Keep Exploring–If You Have More Time!

- Can you match the small bones in owl pellets with comparable human bones that have the same names?

Words to Know

acid—A substance that forms hydrogen ions (H^+) in water and has a pH less than 7.

biome—A region of the earth with a characteristic climate and species of plants and animals.

board foot—A measurement of lumber equal to one square foot with a thickness of one inch.

cast—A shape made by pouring a fluid substance into a mold in which it hardens.

climatogram—A graph that shows annual monthly rainfall and temperature for a particular place on earth, such as a city or town.

conifers—Trees such as cedars, pines, firs, and redwoods that produce cones as a means of reproducing.

deciduous trees—Trees that lose their leaves during cold weather or during a dry season.

density—The mass of a substance divided by its volume. For example, the density of water is one gram per milliliter.

evaporation—The change of a liquid to a gas.

insulator—A material that slows the flow of heat.

melting point—The temperature at which a substance changes from a solid to a liquid. The melting point of ice or snow is 0°C or 32°F.

midday—The time when the sun is highest in the sky and is due south of an observer.

owl pellets—Undigested food, mostly hair and bones, regurgitated by owls.

permafrost—A thick layer of soil that is permanently frozen.

pressure—A force acting on an area. Pressure is defined as force per area or a force divided by the area on which it acts. For example, air pressure is about 15 pounds per square inch.

solar altitude—The sun's angle above the horizon.

solar energy—Light energy provided by the sun.

Further Reading

Bardhan-Quallen, Sudipta. *Championship Science Fair Projects: 100 Sure-to-Win Experiments*. New York: Sterling, 2005.

Davis, Barbara. *Biomes and Ecosystems*. Milwaukee: Gareth Stevens Publishers, 2007.

Day, Trevor. *Taiga*. Chicago: Raintree, 2010.

Guiberson, Brenda Z. *Life in the Boreal Forest*. New York: Henry Holt, 2009.

Latham, Donna. *Amazing Biome Projects You Can Build Yourself*. White River Junction, Vt.: Nomad Press, 2009.

Rhatigan, Joe, and Rain Newcomb. *Prize-Winning Science Fair Projects for Curious Kids*. New York: Lark Books, 2006.

Internet Addresses

Science for Kids: Taiga Forest Biome

http://www.ducksters.com/science/ecosystems/taiga_forest_biome.php

Taiga

http://www.blueplanetbiomes.org/taiga.htm

Answer to page 25 question: **The snow is on the north side of the house.**

Index